# More Light

# More Light

## Hilary Clark

A clever reader is someone who understands squiggles and spots of ink written in what looks like secret messages.

The clever reader that belongs to this book is :

Nathan Haims

Brick Books

CANADIAN CATALOGUING IN PUBLICATION DATA

Clark, Hilary Anne, 1955–
More light

Poems.
ISBN 0-919626-98-X

I. Title.

PS8555.L363M67 1998 C811'.54 C98-932604-7
PR9199.3.C52M67 1998

We acknowledge the support of the Canada Council for the Arts for
our publishing programme. The support of the Ontario Arts
Council is also gratefully acknowledged.

The cover is after a painting by Catherine Macaulay,
*Primula Veris*, watercolour on paper, 28 x 38 cm., 1997.

Typeset in Ehrhardt.
The stock is acid-free Zephyr Antique laid.
Printed and bound by The Porcupine's Quill Inc.

Brick Books
431 Boler Road, Box 20081
London, Ontario, N6K 4G6

brick.books@sympatico.ca

In memory of Cathy Funk


and of my grandmothers
Winifred Clark
&
Margery Gartside

# Contents

One

# The Memory of Words

# Fetish

*clay, feather*

*bone antler*

*turquoise*

*coral*

*shell*

*serpentine*

*chalcedony          alabaster*

*cornpollen*

wet brick, stiff, a fetish stick
the dead moist and cool underground

barb and shaft lodged in the flesh
nest scent, path of least resistance

branched horn of the male, whalebone,
ivory, the elk's exquisite rib

cloudy sky, one milk-green stone
in autumn a flowering in secret places

pink polyps, the baby cuts new teeth
*corallum*, tender pith of love

slow whorl, stripped husk –
tongue soft as a mollusc, and singing

sinuous, the ductile skin of words
red scales, fins, shadows swimming

apple-green – a woman's mind is light,
a shattered crystal, tears

corn dust rising in the sun

# Hypnos

an onrush, flowing, gathering debris   world's prose, crows
strung along a telephone wire, crickets in the long dry grass

a creaky song of ghosts and husks   your voice,
this wind singing through the grass, *hypnos*, spoken

aghast, afflicted by the beauty of words,
apparitions, auras in the dictionary   *haunting, havoc*
summer's disorder

ghostwriter in the memory of words, remnants
of a body deeply loved   *hawthorn*, sweet in leaf, but sharp
*hollyhock*   resisting skin of the world

# Tomato

Eat it, snuff it, cup it. *Pomodoro*, the word rolls off the tongue, pulp, seeds and all. Golden apple spurt. Little pumpkin. Red ruddy rotund, fall fires and the days quickly darkening. One perfect blemish, one shadow, elongating. Open. Flesh, the soft parts of bodies frighten me, vegetable animal, inner water. Cut, the rim of skin remains red; paler tissue, cloud of juice or albumen. Whiter veins branch, disappear; lakes open. (Faint smell of sour earth, salt.) Greenish slime sac, amniotic, tomato babies cluster and wait. Faint spines cross our vision, fetal extensions. The heart at the rot of it. Loveapple, skin closing over. Two wet seeds on a white plate.

In a cupped hand. *Pomodoro*, rain roll, confusion of tongues and flesh. Fish to spawn, apple spurge, acid. Lemon pumpkin. Egg rind, bloody, and feverish fleeing days. One pale long shadow sully. Perfect. Open. Coral granulation; larvae in a soft brush with water. Cut, the skin remains a lip, delicate. A 'mystical dream' of birds, insects, druid horsemen. Fluid humour between skin and the edible part of the embryo. Snow lung alveolar; a honeycomb of alpine lakes. Bitter, run to earth. On the dark side of the moon, a sea, amniotic limbs. Nonetheless, we keep from falling. Effete, a worm in the mouth. Knuckled up.

Flowering vessel, bones and wire. The clickclicking of metal balls. Grenades explode, rain, falling pulp of apples and fish. Human offal, delirium in a bitter egg. We eat our own flesh and lemon, flee our acid shadows. Open. Pink polyps, an island of polished teeth. In the bath, she arranges her toys in tribes. Flayed, the skin is very thin. Passing through water, fern vertebrae, vetch. Define: think like an insect. Bitten, liquid: the baby was hungry even before birth. By the pond, breath freezes into crystals, rice; white hair tangles in the trees. Distant baying in the fog – a lighthouse cornered by sperm-flecked whales. Given sin, we flourish, taking in the view.

4

A bitter knuckle. Caught red-handed in soft chuckle mickle silk, ruby and blossom and dust. Flesh *au meunière*, the miller's wife catches cockchafers, the fine white eggs of ecstasy. We duck our sun outlines, blood mines, prophetic. A lacework, alack. Open. Colonies of blue fern furl, uneasy. In the cage, she places bells, a cuttlefish. Polished, the skin chips off in little bits. Within, a sea; bones cross in a cloud of invisible ink. Refine time. A horseman chortles by the shore, his mane transparent in the breeze. Glut so close, so sweet.

5

Where the words bite, we bleed. *Wermod*, a bitter tonic. Hands set free a cloud of arsenic, copper mullets, roses and tears. We eat too much, aching after one big idea. Cod, coptic matter. Porous. Baked in the earth with tomatoes, flaming heads. We meet our own shadows among the foxgloves, hearts racing among heliotropes. Some septic matter, precious – orange sporangium, vessel of love. We sleep too much, hissing. Struck, she opens her mouth to the god. Eyes to the estuary, ribs red and broken. Warmed by the breath, the first blue milk. Salt. The tongue is a truculent lover.

Intelligence, split distinctions. In each seed, a smaller worm carrying a seed. Hot bluff but wind at the flash of a gun. Yellow forsythia, wool and dust; snuff after love. Logic, the ligament of thought. The spikes opened holes for fluid to pass. She has toothache, delusions of light and swift change. Her fingers dissemble, find spots on a leaf. Sacramental, knowing the water sign, deep green syringa, blood. We are suspended over the flood. Iris, sea *baleine*. The sun licks the first wild hyacinths. Glass. I am wrapped in the humour of your eye.

Quick. Quiet. The loaf is cloven, fragrant cake. In every oyster a stone. Red roe. She nestles the windfalls in her skirts. Borders of poisonous ovules; pollen clings to her hands. A civet sneaks under the bush. Fear, the musk of thought. A compulsion to open holes, read flesh in mystic shorthand. She has toothache, hard dense lumps under pink gums. Will wisdom be gold, silver, salmon, very thin – or winged? Fervent, knowing fire, the glowing coal. Lips blow the blossoms home. Orange, a bruised blue. The Hyades dip below a rolling sea. Withdraw your fingers, glistening. I am rising.

# Basho's Dream

In a lost year,
*I left my broken house*, awaiting
a sign, sore wind blowing,
my heart torn in the clouds, blowing.

I am no priest, dust clings to my feet.
Then, I sought only
surrender,
the small child lovely,
sweet as clover in my arms.

*A line of smoke, morning tea,*
moon still hanging in the sky.
The gate of the garden was open
to the child, closed
to me.
       In the outer shrine
I composed a poem on white silk,
counting butterflies, ivy leaves
climbing the wall.

Afternoon slipped into night.
I opened my eyes.
There, under the wall
*a woman was washing potatoes,*
skins pale in the dusky light.
I fingered the beads in my palm,
the child half-asleep,
softly breathing.

*On the road to the deep north*
I found my life, bitter herbs
my mother grew, a few grey hairs.
Walking away, I encountered myself.
The child, though cold, was radiant,
sleeping under divine protection.

In the mountains, ancient poets
took tea in the *smoky rain.*
The child woke to bells like small rain
and we washed in the half-light,
happy.

*At the end of a long dream of peonies*, snow fish,
the restless, yearning dead,
I lay on my grass pillow
eating rice-cakes, praising the gods.
Ducks flew overhead
and the years, the years
in their wake.

At Nara, spring broke.
The plum tree, indifferent,
dropped blossoms on my head.
The child carried *a branch of wild azalea*,
her face turning pink at my touch.

Spirits in their house of love,
wild sparrows perched on a bucket.
Counting the lice on my black robes,
I pondered the full moon, *Buddha-
after-enlightenment.*
                    Purple clover,
the child silent, crouched
in the summer grass.

*It is the drifting clouds* that mark
my vocation – bamboo in the wind,
little puddles of light.
The art of poetry uncertain –
animal mind, moon
mind, such illusions.

In October we ascended the river,
the *thin drapery* of a life
torn away.

The child dropped crumbs
overboard, fed them to the fish.

The cuckoo sang in the gathering rain.

# Swallows

Thought hovers, buoyed, skipping without colour

Swallows build mudnests, dive from eaves
on billows of their own making

Nothing soothes the hunger, no dam
against the past

How translate the musk of summer grass,
the dust wet with showers

Joy is an emptiness, light,
suspended
                your lovely face consumed by rain

# Luminous

## The Interval

In the dawn watch, a mirror
catches our faces        confused,
swimming into light

                    perfection
this interval, lapse
between moments

In their beds, the children are still,
pale as moths

what transient clarity
in a face –

a few first notes by ear
close – hist
                    dispersed

## Speak

Broken, breathless    caught up
in a sage wind, sea
of stars

heart brought to
a polish
                cracked

vibrato     soft, soft
against glass

       tremulous
testing the limit of sound

a small tongue, persistent
and I
     a bruised reed

# A Message

Carnal, bruised, tongues struggle
in the dark      language a real
yet resisting presence

A small light persists      but clouds,
motes in the eye

Tricked by your hands, I stayed
but only just      the house reeling
between us      world beyond our walls
inconsequential
                    even the rubbish piled high
stench of shit, rotting fruit
        great holes in the road
it all
        fell away –

I want to tell you      simply

the wind was potent
one blow to the chest and a life opened
clean
        thin column of smoke,
white bodies of moths
                    I want to tell you this
before the clarity is gone

for I have never touched without your tongue,
tasted without your hands      you,
circling even my sleep

                        yet that wind
was *my* breath, now a mere whisper

                              want to say —


I want to say      the night was alive with wings
cool hands, tongues
of messengers

                  the others who seek us
and rest grieving

            upon our brokenness

# Ça

Swanfeathers on a white mantel,
the pale heart turns again      in winter

the sun is flat, unsymbolic      mind leans
into composition      moth dance, light

an edge receding      door unhinged
a dark sliding in      some scent of loss
or sweetness

*And amorous*, the mind is
taken      sweet pea, the hybrid colours
of longing      mauve, yellow, cream

the beatitude of a moth circling
upon its own being      light, more light
risking perfection

Tongues touch, ça, ça      and burnt,
one relearns each small
daily pleasure

angel of illumination caught
between two swanfeathers

on the wing of a kiss      turning

# Riddle

Flutters over picket fences, skirting
temptation      a dim white face, nocturnal

Throws itself at the idea of light, its
sensation       hovers fitfully over sickles and hoes

Membranous, mind a pliable fold,
nervure      moonlight veining its wings

Given to morbid excitement      tonguing
night windows, nibbling lingerie on the washline

Its desire a thin skin overlaid with green
flame      a blind touch, igniting

or fooled by falling stars, the luminous drift
of meaning      a mind in scattered pieces,
a poem's undress

# Dance

Sweet bergamot, reddish light-spill
on hands      grief keens its love –
*all one, all one –*
                    reason stumbles
before the world.


September apples, cold, a wind
shakes the boughs
                    I am falling
toward a place below water,
the last light vanishing
over my head.


Dark glass, its polish –

                    quick, unfettered,
the dance, shadows in a whirlpool, the
thrust –


heart caught in its own snare,
laughing.

Two

# Beloved

~

# Eros

*for Tim Lilburn*

When desire opens wide as the sky
heavens, blue meteors, stars showering on your head

when it writes every word and the spaces between words
curling the commas, commas, commas      punctual –
skidding to a provisional halt

then away with the swallows, up to the eaves
a fine down licked by a wind more urgent than breathing

erotic, elliptic, slipping into melancholy      madness
of 4am, basho's *narrow road*,
reading words that multiply      rise off the page like smoke, errant

erring      watched with mounting concern by friars,
madonnas, gods nailed helplessly to crucifixes

following saint francis through the long silky grass
waxwings and finches hovering over his hands

the desire of a plover encountering its own smooth belly
reflected in a slough

when there is not enough time, when love swallows the minutes,
tipsy     a gathering storm of unknowing

and you watch the smooth glass of the poem ripple
just a breath
                    a face flowing, changing
at your touch.

# All Our Words Blow One Way

sun splashes sacraments over glass and ice, sharp wind and the immolation of desire. all our words blow one way, skittering. the frozen ground sings underfoot. breathless, we fly after weather-cocks spinning in wild, operatic gusts. this is how the work begins, in the mingled water and wine that pours glittering from water-spouts, the sun on our bare heads. farce and sacrifice, our angelic nature clumsy, impure. buffoons brawl in the rowan tree, we should know, we've been there, punch drunk and crying out for grace

all our words lit from within. spirit rides a wave of annihilation, flirting, stung by desiring tongues. this is how the work begins, in the loving trickery of syllables, new wine effervescing, overflowing its cups. composing the fiery heart, fingers singed and winged. tipplers sing in the rowan tree, ecstatic, crying a new millennium.

# Edge

Bookends, look: imagine two black swans
or saints, constriction of the feathered heart.

In the shadow before dawn, furtive beaks,
a nest woven of cries, scraps of anguish.

Listen – voices, my ear to the wind, white-
throat singing *laughter, laughter.*

It's spring, there are shears in your gloved hands.
Love scissors between us, earthstained, hungry.

A lilac veiled with green blood: imagine lilies
opening to your touch, your lovely, darting tongue.

# Secret Gardens

Of secret gardens,
green tracery in the vein.

In May, the tulips utter little pink
screams. The first mosquitoes proceed
quietly, just the faintest
moans, invisible wounds
opening to the light.

The river glistens under a warm aura of sewage.

Landscaped gardens, green stigmata.
Buds weep chloral blood
and from the bark a breathing –
all the puppies in the neighbourhood piss
on the angel's beautiful, polished skin
and the sparrows pause in her arms.

Francis of Assisi wears the marks of the elect –
bird droppings, petals,
spores, cloudy tears.
Cracks web his stony skin, nose
blown away by a fatal wind.

Roses open their mouths
brushed by a wing, proboscis, tongue –

a ripple wind, mind's inflorescence.
Cats pause, lost in their washing.

At times the gardens in your mind
form one green story: St. Francis with his birds,
marble angels, a flowering apple,
calico cats sitting zen.
Sister moon perched briefly
in your hands.

How fine, the light of her countenance.

Gulls, camellias scatter
in a white sea wind.
This light, this bread, broken
wings.

# A Garden

Mozart violins, piano softly rocking, little blue horse among cherry leaves. In fall mottle bottle fly. Worms chew and notch folded paper, silver foil. Spore and fern, brown cryptogam. A weather vessel. A mirage of lemon and peach. The little god caresses a dolphin: light on lips, meshed leaf and twig. Sprigged. A limb as shiny as kettles. Sunlight, reeds folded in sharp creases, pressed back by the pressure of invisible bodies. Brother sun, briar rose, round windows onto the sky. A universe so tiny and secret it can't be written. Resistant: seed-pellets, pods, but no birds come. It's a question of accuracy, water's white point at leaf-cusp. Litter clots the boughs, arms weary under the weight. Rosehip, petal water and that drop, that drop, still

       suspended

Slats of light, bright diagonals cross the garden wall. Sometimes the sun is green, and sleeps. Invisible fortresses collapse underfoot, a finger's touch dismantles fibre, spore, seedpod. In a clutter of concrete and cold cherubs, the wind hollows out a nest. Cherry wears a dress, necklaced in twining ivy. This hunger. Scrap, leaf-insect, fragile grid of fear. Crying over rusty buckets. Resphighi on the waters, one pale cold rose. The mind is a bud; it trembles on the breeze. The only birds heard are on the radio, a summer music, sad and distant. Sporangia, tiny vessels alight on your hands. Leaves pierced with blades of light, a life askew.

3

Notes on an ascending scale. Green grid, contained infinity: the mind shifts on a breath of air. A life reduced to clods, rippled surd. Ferns expire in a pool of rusting ink. Cherry bends under a weight of butterflies, bowties, blind men's canes. Webs of kitchen string, a clumsy knot under each branch. Dvořák sweeps like wind over the wall. Snubnosed cupid bares his bum, fondles a dolphin. Radio static forms icicles under the wires. In another year, the ivy will reach the top of the tree. A whole garden assuming disguises, watching for stray angels. The eye crosses a cloud chequerboard. Reluctant words, relics without buds or thumbs, sudden sun upon this devastation. Crystal, rosehip, quill: a life in a hollow stem. A life snatched up with the hand, and blue.

4

Jollity a young bird. Young white limbs, cherry buds. The tabby brushes snow from moustache and whiskers. Spring messages run godspeed across the garden, and the magnolia bursts its fat fur buttons. Joy spies spotted woodpeckers clinging like insects to a stem. Taptapping, discovering cuts and grubs under the surface of the world. The green gains a little, but wait – winds from all quarters, plunging ships and unpredictable weathers. A child coughs. In the shell of the house next door, hammers start up, a saw. Gunmetal garden, its trees numb under their rubbed pewter skins. Young suckers half furled. Spring vellum, love's tissue licked and scribbled over and over.

## St. Peter's (Ardingly, Sussex)

Summer's morning –
shadows tremble on stone.
Under the folded linen of an angel's robe
we follow the trace of names, death-dates
engraved over our heads.

Dazed with light we reach back.
Genealogies put forth shoots,
flower under our hands
                              grace notes,
tendrils, remnants,
a virgin's face, lineaments
of a terrible love.

Below the murmur of the prayers
a barely audible sighing –
twin girls buried at birth,
mothers and babes curled
in one another's arms, cryptic
spelling of bone, bracelet, dust.

Sunlight pinpoints a saint's thin hand,
a single brilliant rose. Peace,
a whole family lies encrypted
beneath our feet – we shift, kneel
for the litany, *in your mercy
hear us.*

Incense, lilies, *summer's lease* –
a final blessing, raucous laughter
of crows. We rise from the pews
and go out, picking a path
among nettles, green
headstones hot in the sun.

Within, angels hide their faces.
A woman grieves in the stippled light
and something remains under stone,
writing.

# Woman in Doorway (Variations)

Framed by light, a woman in a doorway. Something exposed, whites of eyes. Pressure on the optic nerve, a peculiar illumination: hand rests on doorjamb, a string of perfect pearls. The ticking of the watch strapped to your wrist.

Final letters, an intimate acrostic of nerve and fibre. The woman's profile is cut out of light. Your risky breathing, her eye's lateral slide. A fine neuritis, love draws a halo around her head: impossible, the black doorjamb, buttons on her cuff. Touch, the touch. Heart's secret semaphore.

The writing on her perfumed skin, little missives of spirit. Nervous devotions, the woman's cheek edged with light. Dark iris, the shutter closes upon your gaze; you wait, exhaling. Aura of rose, musk, hand cradling the cranium: on the doorjamb, the glint of her nails. Brushed, just. A private body of grief.

The suicide's vanishing alphabets. xxx. Little poems etched in the skin, the woman's hair threaded with pale ribbons. Lilies in her hands. The eye finally shuts. You breathe in a scent of oleander, secret poison: the doorjamb disappears into light. Bright-eyed; a thousand *torn birds*, keening.

# Testament

*... My mind is running on pure grief*
*and pure love, I want you to know this.*
— Don Coles, 'Forests of the Medieval World'

These things I leave, *my mind running,*
slipping – first light, silver gleam in the east,
Venus wet, twisting back,
night's ocean whispering in the whorl of her ear.
To you I leave the outline of forms,
blue snow under pines, lucid
lettering of needle and sheath,
little deaths, crucifixions in a thornbush.
To you, as well, the winter dark,
its distances – you open the gate
and stars, small broken angels
fall around you.

Fasting, high on *pure grief, pure*
*love*, I plunder the dictionary for gifts.
'Lily': slender madonna, Lenten
tongues, the long pale leaves
of melancholy. Tigerlily, golden
dust. Or 'light': the *optic heart*,
a thin film, shining. In heaven,
a wall of final letters and no–one
reading. And 'love', of course:
bleeding, winged, illegitimate,
the passion of small birds in winter.
A purple thorn, a bloom.

These are my offerings, *I want you to know* –
how night after night, restless,
I toss – how waking at four,
one solitary star shining, I commune
with death, the luminous head appearing,
disappearing, in the glass. *I want you
to know this.* Grieving, drinking off
the dregs, I wait for a sign:
feathers, blood in the eaves,
the fury of small hearts
beating.

# Relinquished

I

On a winter's day, the coming of birds.
February hearts harden to glass.

Slim twigs, catprints: in this clarity,
every last pit, particle
of vision.

Light breaks over trashcans,
muddy vans – epiphanies of loneliness,
the spirit's daily bread.

Crabapples litter the lane, split
wineskins. A branch cracks
in an abandoned garden,
the mountain ash fills with waxwings.

You walk on, the dead curled in your heart
like blackened ferns.

2

Devious mind, its abject tricks.
The soul finds solace where it can,
in the rind of an orange,
bitter seeds.

Afflicted, trace of lips
on the lover's scarred body, subtle
fermentation in boll and leaf.

Relinquished, the will slips
loose – a ceasing-to-be,
a forsaking.

But loss has its consolations:
night wakings, tipsy
laughter of the moon,
the dead with their feathery hands.

3

Winter apples, rust. A thaw.
Cupidity of small beaks, berries splattered,
trashed in the mud.

Intellect, its bittersweet
distinctions.

At sunrise, puddles of water turn to wine.
Drunken spirits collide in the lane,
singing.

Yellow-tipped, a winnowing –
sun's fantail in the east.

A gate creaks –
and you running out with empty hands,
the dead unfurling, amorous,
at every step.

# Prayer

This luminous idiocy, light pouring onto hands, bent head. Behind the holy one, a dark lattice cross-hatched in black ink. Last sleep — empty, calm. The fool communes with god, drawing her stiff shroud about her. Dead moth with folded legs, swept from windowsill to floor – grey breastplate and a small, remote face

a thousand representations of bliss, its cold ecstatic hands, madonna, belladonna contemplating the broken body of the world. The son's hollow chest, small birds, a calendar of miracles. We seek this compassion, vines and fingers interlaced, the breast opening like a nest of ivory boxes. We seek this moon face hovering

death's-head swept up with the dust, a small shadow returning to light. Lunatic mother, pray for us, for the pitiless heart, lilies of annihilation.

# Angels

*for Anne Szumigalski*

I

Most invisible body, the past hovers over our daily gestures. Tar soap, running water, wet hand on the door. In the third season, autumnal, we are visited by angels light as leaves, their faces pocked and blackened by decay. We assume the past like an armour of light, our glass bodies licked by fire. And turn to our reading, marking pages, finding familiar spirits where the lines break, and we raise our heads, wondering.

Most invisible body, angel of shame bathes in kerosene and fire, draws her sari round her blackened face. Leaves turn to smoke and earth, curling in the burning wind. We assume the past, drawing its blue flame about us. And this is the key: that we may find spidery messages where the lines hinge, a few tea leaves, flakes of ash.

* * *

Late in the white night, we are touched by fingers softer than a breath. Something not dead but unformed, a space, some brief pause before words. We turn in our sleep. The moon and its hologram float over the frozen city. In the morning a sudden thaw, and the icicles in the eaves grow cloudy and weep. We shut the front door, kiss, and go our separate ways, treading carefully, walking into the unspoken.

2

You turn on the computer, spectral letters floating up from invisible rooms. Quiet murmur, speech turned inward. Its memory has always anticipated you, you are a minor disturbance of its perfection, nothing more.

Troubled, wanting to write about angels, you think of that hawk earlier, worrying the air overhead. You walked awkwardly through the long grass, fearing it, the hawk joining others screaming overhead.

*There may be as many varieties of angels as of birds.* You wish to write a clever natural history (field angels, sea angels) but something begins to break in – your true familiar, memory. Sullen angel who visits you late at night before sleeping, in the interval between waking at dawn and the last, exhausted dream. Who visits in the slough of the afternoon, as you doze over a book. You come up behind her as you write, dogging her key by key, word by word, until she turns –

but you cannot see her face, or not clearly, and you digress, doodling through the dictionary. White angel of distraction, black angel of spleen. Green angel stinking of stilton. Red angel flicking a fox's tail. Blue angel leaning on a doorpost, smoking

tiny bird-bellied angels swoop from the eaves as you lift your eyes and see her watching you, your twin angel gazing at you as you gaze, writing as you write, her poems unfolding like children's paper snowflakes and you remember her hands pulling you into the light, a presence unspeakably familiar, hands stroking your skin, feeding you. Angel of sugar, angel of milk blue as melting ice. Something shivers and cracks, you're on dangerous ground, she grows pale and vanishes among her snowflakes

white letters floating up from darkened rooms. You press save, turn off the machine and in the sudden silence hear crickets, their broken song.

3

FIRST LESSON: Wishing himself dead, Elijah said, 'It is enough,' and slept. But the angel wasn't having any of it, hauled him up and barked, 'Eat', pointing to a cake baked on hot stones, a jar of water. Elijah ate and drank reluctantly, curled up with a great sigh to sleep. But the angel slapped him out of it, ordered him to eat again. His gorge rising, Elijah forced down another cake, more water, and stumbled off on his journey (forty long days and nights) to Horeb, mountain of God. The angel absentmindedly pointing the way.

HOMILY: Now why do angels so often appear in sleep, or on the feathered edge of sleep? Silvered, iridescent, they might seem to be mere creatures of the dreaming brain, delicious disturbances of the electric aura, subtle emanations (rose, honeysuckle) of the erotic lobes. But no, oh no they are *real* – fireflies, ardent spirits pursuing us, weaving their luminous envelope around us. Angels stand glowing at the crossroads of life, beckoning to each of us: in our lesson, the angel draws the prophet inward, into the most intimate recesses of the soul; and so does the 'still small voice' of God whisper to us when, deep in the night, we reach Horeb, and surrender to the mighty wind, the earthquake, and the fire. As well, Yahweh's lovely messengers bring us spiritual food, which we refuse to our great loss. Elijah's angel offers him a simple cake, but this cake, too, is spiritual nourishment. 'Take, eat, this is my body': can we not hear our Lord's tempting words when the angel invites Elijah to eat not one but two sweet cakes baked on hot stones? Is there not, then, a foreshadowing of 'Drink this, all of you', the chalice of precious blood still, here, a jar of pure water that quenches the prophet's thirst, cools his swollen tongue? Like Elijah, we need this divine sustenance, this manna, if we are to walk forth, day by weary day, on our own journeys, our forty days and forty nights in the bleak desert, watching, waiting for messengers, those dark raptors, oh! coming after –

SILENT REFLECTION: eat me drink me mmmm alice's little seed cake bottle of cordial tasting of toffee, turkey and hot buttered toast falling asleep she fell down a rabbit hole a bossy white angel with pink eyes waistcoat and a pocket watch was her undoing

'angel at the crossroads' who or what *was* that by my bed the other night as I lay half-asleep he's right about the erotic lobes a faint scent of rose skin like silk or is it milk I dreamed of eating at a table laden with fruit biting into kumquats figs the apricots had a slight tang or was it a first whiff of rot I ate and ate till I was ready to burst woke up feeling sick and that scent, stale, still in the air

and on to our journey in the wilderness etcetera Elijah's jar of cool water didn't Christ say I thirst I remember as a child dipping my paintbrush into a jar of fresh water turning it pink or blue or green after a while a brown sludge but before that in the newness of the colours I would paint angels their hems and wings wet touched with light

4

White morning      sheer curtains gust out
writing, you are drawn to devotions
contemplation      hungry for form, its spacious rooms
angels floating, rapt, in the corridors

This is the poem, thinking      her face indistinct
stippled with half-shadow, sun
as one, waking from the dead, said
to the woman      do not touch me, I am not yet
home      the poem is only half-born
emerging from the tomb, blue light of desire

On the other side of music
on the other side of sleep      a fine rain falls
wetting eyelash, pale cheek      you move to touch
her face, it is your face      new
yet utterly familiar

Milk, breath      skin brushing skin
slow love, its wet caress
the child smiles in the loveliness
and her face comes closer, wondering

As he said to the woman      go, tell the others
so you kiss her face      turn
and enter the form      that house
you have been building, always, within you
preparing a place for the others

# Beloved

The heart swarms with fervent birds,
chickadees, each with its small black cap
of abnegation.

Diamonds in the gut, a hunger sharper
than shining pins. Snow,
a few precious crumbs.

You remember the rainforest
         young bracken, huckleberries,
succulent tongues singing the green
heat, mossy body of plenitude.

Now, in a prairie garden, ghosts
parsing illegible sentences in the snow.
You stand among them
emptyhanded
              stars
forming flowers,
fluid ideograms above you.

Heaven on earth, a sparrow's
thought larger than logic.
Carnal constellations, the ram,
the archer
            stars,
lucid crystals
and that body, beloved,
under your feet.

Loving her white belly, luminous
cave of ice    thighs, pubis
of fern, curled leaf
                    ghosts
descend on her breasts and you turn,
listening for the millennium.

# Quickening

March wind, and the cold
is a corset of bones.
The river grinds its teeth,
moaning
        bitter crystals,
miracles forming before you.

Invisible mind, its chill
striations
        a necklet of icicles
melting one by one.

Cracked, flawed –
you might be happy, just,
in the sun's touch
        water singing
beneath the river's ridged skin.

2

*And when this perishable body
has been clothed*, ghosts will rise
from the river, crying – why
did you leave us, why
is love dissolution
                    our end
and bitter joy?

The words of the beloved
are full of grace
                    a garment
shining in the sun –
sparrows pecking at its hem,
nesting in its sleeves –
                    spring's quickening
and the coming thaw.

# Three

# Ghosts

## White Nights

night after night a light burns in your window     you are holding up words like small, glowing eggs     the child nestled in your heart stirs, but is silent     no word will do, you imagine a room as cold and empty as the page before you     blank walls, snowdrifts through the open window, *sanctus,* one substance, now and forever this loss     witless, a child shivering in the street     you imagine, in this white room, a vase holding a single iris, purple-black turning the page, turning it back, you glimpse a trace folded into the golden sex of the flower     light slants across your feet, you stand listening to the child, its cry low but growing     broken egg-shells, the page glows under your fingers and briefly the body, loved, prismatic

in the morning shining waxwings will beat at your window     *and the clamour of inchoate birds*

# Fable

This is the first story: a boy, a girl, a forest,
a path but no way home.

You remember waking famished for love, no bread
in the house and a cold new year.

Or a surfeit for the solstice, sugar dusting
the eaves, ice sweet against teeth;
inside a singing and moaning from the oven

and you can't go back – silent, watchful,
the snow swallows up the evidence.

A quiet house, just you sucking mints.
Outside, the children's footsteps fill.

Little sparrow on the washline      oh, sweet
frozen heart.

# Light Narratives

She was sliding her finger into a socket, slipping a radio into the bath. Her hands were water, her body transparent as love. She opened her eyes; she knew from the dream something had moved. In the air a dim halo remained. Who was that woman raising her hand. Would there be time to warn them before all the closet doors flew open, before the house broke open in the light –

\* \* \*

A woman's hand rests on the switch. At the corner of the mantel, forbidden matches in a blue glass jar. A Chinese iron, a set of Dickens. The child, curled, strains to hear the TV's inaudible music. Goodnight moon, the fire dies. A little knitting, silver pressure on the eastern windows.

Streaks like beams of the sun, there is order in our rising.

\* \* \*

When she was a girl, she read Alice, became Alice with poker face and pointed rodent feet. Reading, she followed the diminishing line of words to the end of the curly mousetail. Was there light at the end of the spiral, at the bottom of the sea of tears?  Would she ever get home? Would she turn back at the wet rosebushes?  Slap of brush, smell of paint, sound of approaching footsteps –

\* \* \*

Long, tentative days. She wiped the sunny window with a rag, looked out to the tiny freighters clinging to the Point. Sparrows took a bath as the first odd drops fell to earth. The lawnmower clattered into the shed. If she had the house to herself she would walk around all the rooms, sit in each, leaving a pen, a newspaper, haircombs, two warmed earrings to mark her spot. But there were others. She could hear a kettle boiling somewhere, the click of a thermostat, a cough. She remained at the window, rubbing a spot clear.

\* \* \*

With what relinquished. Caught in the intimate weft of breath and loving. She slouched by the tub and ate an apple. A life composed from meal to meal, bath to bath, sleep to sleep. What could she retain of this carnal punctuation: a bite, a kiss, a final punch to the pillow, a shove to the sleeper straddling the bed. Power an inaudible rhythm, circuitry – could she enter the room, and speak –

\* \* \*

She was coming closer. Dangerous objects: glossy men's magazines under wraps, cars with their hoods up in oil-stained garages, chopping knives – anything lethal, metallic, and fine. Circular saw, slim drill. She hesitated before picking up the hand mixer, holding it far away – light glancing off its blades – then close, closer. To lose a finger would be an initiation, she thought, ejecting the blades with a clatter into the sink. Her hand felt for the switch.

In mind

　　　　this supple instrument, mercy


You climb out of the law, you begin to flame.

# Opal

## Sunroom

A pattern of light, a mind.

Through the cracked glass, maple spinners and bleeding stems. Cushioned, I recline with *Rasselas*, the baby knocking softly in my belly. Streaked reflections, branches on an inner window. The day-bed creaks. A line of ants crosses the sill, climbs the doorframe, disappears.

Small, I would peer through the keyhole. Binoculars hung in their leather case by the door. Beyond the tall hedge, a white house, the sea. Cloud-world flux and roll, sea-ceiling. She served muffins, spotted cheddar, tea. Hand with its opal ring, colours changing to green and rose.

Amiss, it's all. Altered. Mouldy crusts, chickadees suddenly quiet in the feeder. A storm blows up at night, flagstones wet, lights slick on the steps. Her gloved hand pausing at the gate.

## White Bedroom

A shadow falls on the wall. My bed floats over hers. A pattern of light – water, sun, chequered leaves. She would stand at the dresser mirror brushing out her steely hair. Sparks. Putting on her rings – opal, pearl. In her jewelbox, a glass eye, gold filling. Now, curled in labour, breathing, I listen to the rain and the digging outside, spade through earth striking stone.

Mirror draws long light on the door. Lakes for sleep. She would lie, tapping her cold fingers on the counterpane. Nightbirth, a relentless dilation. No turning back –

rose, bitter grain

green

## Red Bedroom

When I was a child, I knew when not to speak. I stuffed my dolls in her peg bag, read the *Just-So Stories*, Hitchcock's *Fearful Tales*. Arranged coloured spools in her sewing drawer, fingering the tomato pincushion with its tiny strawberry, the slim paper packets of needles. The wardrobe in the red bedroom had a peephole shaped like a cloverleaf, a tunnel to Narnia. Curled in the top bunk, I would sail the night waves. Beyond the curtain, tugs in the starry harbour.

Now I curl under hospital sheets, recovering, and again something deeper, danger, silence. My son lies crying in an oxygen box with holes for rubber hands. As they carried her in, dying, on a stretcher, she asked for a gin and tonic

opal ring, horned thumbnail, sheen of fly wing

wires, my fluids (hers, baby's) in tubes, circuit of lipids, colostrum, blood. Crow in the road goes for the jugular, the long blue vein. Little bird. The baby's chest was pierced, blood and water, vital fluids, flesh lashed with cords and thorns.

## Paraclete

The spirit speaks from the flame throats of flowers, whispers that death shoves, whiteknuckles its way out of the ground. The smell of freesias around my hospital bed – a surfeit, sweet. Fetus at rest, curled in an incubator; oxygen blossoms rich and growing. Eventually he uncurled and grew, snatching at his respirator, feeding tubes. The guardians emptied the flower jar, pouring the green murk and stems away. Milk was flowing, nights blue and shining on a new child

irises, stars on the sea

Spring pleads perpetually, *would it be, would it be*
out of the throats of the dying.

## Living Room

Good Friday. *I count my bones.* Having entered her house, I will never leave. Chairs arranged just so: two little ones for you, a rocker for me. A shadow falls on the wall. Rusty the Rooster nods sleepily in his peg bag, drops a picture book, *The Borrowers*. A child in a mahogany cabinet, breathing.

First the mantel clock would chime, then the echo, then the fear. She was silent as the dust motes erasing the window. Just Pod, and Homily, and little Arietty. She would flex her knuckles, the light catching her opal ring. Jade, cloud of pink dogwood through the window. A leaning tower of books. Was she really reading that thriller or was she looking at me. Hands deep in a mending bag: stone, needle, amber beads. Then the grandfather clock would strike, then raindrops on the glass. 3 o'clock. Now, walking a fretful baby, pacing, I count the steps to the dogwood, the light.

## Kitchen

In the photograph, a little girl stands at the sink holding a shining tin teapot. The window is a pattern of light. Maple spinners toss on a stream of wind. The girl is pouring the water into small ceramic bowls the colour of butter. A whole world flowing in at her eyes.

Once, near the end, we opened the door and found her alone in the kitchen lit by blue fluorescent tubes. She was grilling a cheese sandwich, her opal knuckle knocking the black skillet. The radio was playing Elgar or Bach. When we left, she stood on the back step, waving under the hanging stockings and stays. Then stepped back into the light.

*My love dwelt in a northern land.* I wait for her, watching the children grow, while in the photo the little girl pours water endlessly from teapot to bowl, and an old woman looks up, startled, at the door.

# Cellar

A dream of children, transparent, rising through the windows.

In the cellar, a cupboard door that's rarely opened. Cardboard, splintered plywood, fingers cold on the lock. Crushed coal on the ground, black footprints. A shadow falls on the wall, on an old pink map of Canada. Cobwebs. Behind the cracked pane, a squirrel's grey face.

The cellar was always silent. Leaning towers of cigarette tins (green Export A, yellow Sportsman) held nails, screws, buttons, fishhooks, lures. The cupboards with the Drano and solvents had white faces. Flies beat and beat on the glass. Dusty pickle jars stuffed with stiff brushes; greasy tins of turpentine, linseed oil. I stayed out of the spidery corners. Her foot would pause on the step.

If I draw her face in the dust, if I rest my cheek on stone –

## Opal

A bird sings at midnight. Somewhere a baby stirs. This is her body, its changing light and shadow.

Mexican silver and turquoise in a tinderbox, rose jellies in a blue glass jar. Dresser drawers: two peeling bibles, a string of discoloured pearls, an opal ring. Pantry: decanters of sherry, port, rusting tins of peas and corn. When we finally clear out the house we open all the cupboards to air. Rags and clothespins, lemon oil, dusty bottles of ginger beer. I pull long steely hairs from the folding ironing board, the wringer washer. I am afraid to stay in the house alone. Yellowing stays and stockings she hung on the back line, her hands with raised veins, my hand in hers and a faint blue cord knotting from knuckle to soft crook of arm.

sun, hummingbird
       light

# Small Shadows

*Une étrangère s'est glissée dans mes paroles...*
— Philippe Jaccottet, 'A la lumière d'hiver'

Suffering the ides of spring,
its cold tongue.

Moans from the ocean, my words
wounded, the shards
of that body, that stranger enfolding me
as I write
      lines scratched on glass,
small shadows against the coming light.

A hand slips into my dream,
halting
      icicles melt
along the eaves, and I wake
tasting blood.

Broken vowels, the crazed
ice skin of puddle under boot
      briefly a face, shattered, wet
with tears.

Her tongue in my mouth is sweet
and cold
      tasting privation,
syllables of skin and longing.

Just a semblance, ghost of light
beyond the line
                    spring tide,
the new moon weightless
in my arms.

# Her

You might pause, looking again at the snow beneath your feet – flecked ice a mica, silvered – tasting the granular cold on the tongue. *As if a single image*, ice reflecting streetlights on a January morning, clouded breath rising like saints, pale, venerated – as if a semblance could suffice. You and your counterpart, walking as bicycles skid past, as traffic rumbles blindly over the bridge, snowflakes caught in every headlight. She looks at you once, then disappears around the next corner. A smile glimpsed in the glass, the very form of desire. Illusions, *the wheat the sea the mountain*, warm skin and limbs relinquished. Imagine her now in the next street, head bowed against the cold, waiting for the signal. Imagine the light or love wrapped about her. As if thinking *were enough to set off the trembling*. You walk on, bicycles, cars, a few last stars swimming in the crazy optic of your tears.

2

Imagine her now, the raw lilies unfurling in her throat, their scent and fleshy thrust. Imagine the poison burning a path through esophagus to gut. Choking on blood and bile, cruel wings bearing down. And now we sit, ten years later, and *hesitate between orchid and star*, trying to evoke that flower in her throat, so beautiful, desired and deadly. Lilies in the rain, the relentless downpour of November in Vancouver, dead leaves clogging the stormsewers. At her funeral, *even the eyelids cast shadows*. A thousand candles could not illumine her grief, hold back that final, terrible dark. A mouth consumes us, we are swept up in unknowing. On the street, people will never suspect the illusion of our slow bodies, *hushed voices*. We are not here. We have entered a desire as pure as an orchid, as fatal as a star. Catherine, on your fiery wheel, forgive us.

## 3

In the story you tell your children each night, a woman walks into the sea. She is singing and her skin is green. Sunset clouds piled high, red sky. The youngest child curls against you, *reciting in a hushed voice* the sacred words: 'Her lips, her lungs, cold seaweed in her hair.' You turn your ear inward, hearing her song, tasting the salt on her skin. Large mind, *translating its oceans.* She is the spit in your children's mouths, their fevers and midnight voyages. She is the words that arrive unsought, wet with brine. The older ones take up the refrain: 'O mother, lay us down in the arms of the sea.' And climb the stairs to their beds and windlashed dreams. In the dark, you imagine *a painting ... that would be only a luminous vanishing point*, a skiff disappearing over the horizon, wet heads in the waves and something singing, *crying out* from the deep.

## 4

'Halo,' 'corona,' 'areola' – the light of a word can circle a life. Illumination from the heart to the skin, *the weeping flesh*, its imperfections. This morning 'moon' in her hands, a gift. A world incorporated with words, each day a new wafer dissolving on the tongue. This is her body, in remembrance. *Depending on the light of the season*, ghosts arrive to haunt heart and marrow. White hands in mudra, meditating. One might say this mantra – abide-in-me – forever, word reverberating on the threshold of sleep. The sea sounds in memory, her feet just brushing the water, bluish-green and algae bleeding at her touch. *A single word* and she will come to you, ringed with light, as netfuls of fish are pulled from the sea.

# Woman Bathing

Bird of paradise, spiked
jet crest and blood-red gorge.
This is your birthday, flowers
gathered from the slopes of Hale Akela.

You rise early, walk in shallows
already warmed by the morning sun.
Migratory birds fall stunned
at your feet.

Your beautiful blue breast flares
as the sun climbs to the meridian,
and white sharks bask
in the surf.

Shells, small vertebrae, auguries –
you clean the fine sand from your feet,
Juno among her peacocks, eyes wide,
scanning an ocellated sea.

Your mind is on fire –

iridescent fish fly, hooked,
into the ocean's throat.

# Falling

To fall as lambs are born, into the world.

At forty, a woman falls with a sigh
into her flesh, its heavy grace.

Cast out of heaven, the angels fell heels
over heels, their lucid love in pieces.

To fall on the sword of the moment, oh
holding, letting go –

In the middle of this life, broken,
I stumble on a poem so clear it screams

and temptation like the rain that falls
on the river     warm, staining face and tongue.

## Mud and Spittle

In the unreal TV light, a leprous wife wipes her eyes with her sari's edge, tucking her knobby hand away. The gaze of the clinicians does not miss one oozing wound, one iota of grief. Her family, revolted, will not come to see her. Human refuse, queasy dreams.

Our house is built of bits and scraps, parti-coloured, crazily leaning. Doors and windows mismatched, cupboards gaping, each day the fridge listing further from the wall. The children run into the kitchen and slide. Hounddog in the next yard bays at ghosts, cats collide in showers of sparks. We find our way around by routine, the daily braille of survival. At night, children tucked in their beds, the house slips on its foundations still more. The moon just touches a woman weeping –

we must live in this house we have made, lives leaning, vital papers in sad, dusty piles. Flawed, the heart persists regardless. A little boy straight and sound, wild daisies in the lane.

# Storms

Something beats against the screen.
4 am. You rise in the summer thunder,
roused by the orange glow in the sky,
the TV left on downstairs.
Static, electric storms in the skull
dark wings beating up, soft,
familiar.

The baby coughs and turns.
In his silence your own breathing –
a rattling, light, at the door
and mosquitoes pick out their tunes,
dancing under the ceiling

mmmm, little piccolos.
In the night, anxiety punctures the skin,
blood-map, your life a thin black thread
snapped

and here a woman, child
in a white nightshirt,
waking dreams,
bodies crying out, falling
narcoleptic, ecstatic –

In storms you court sleep,
seeking in the cool
saliva rain some final discharge
of thought.

# Tsunami

No escape –
you wake in a darkened room,
a hand, hot breath on your cheek.
Blind, you carry the small, clinging body
to bed, return to a dream of fires,
tsunamis, abysmal gulfs, the ground
swelling and splitting underfoot.

A fatal wave, a wind.
Cats scream in the lane, locked
in bitter coupling.
On the dark side of the world, sirens,
flares, the lost ones digging
through the rubble.

Walls of water curve,
some seismic moment – love,
hate, the final heave.
Wrecks break open on the ocean floor.
Something is rising, fear muscling up
irresistible, the cold green swell
of memory. And held in its arms,
swept in a curve from grace
to desolation, you imagine gulls
squalling, dropping something soft,
torn on rocks below.

A scent lost again.
On the dark side of the world
the dead mourn the living, shades
crossing chasms
between waking and sleep.

Tremors, a subtle knowing.
The child crawls into your bed.
Something seethes, a secret
combustion. You sleep,
words burning in your mouth.

# Frost

Tracing the heart's circle, body's persistent grief.
Threaded silk, desire of the turning worm,
invisible moth.

*Longueurs* of early afternoon. Feigning regret, the elms dispatch
their startled leaves. You read on the tail of some inner wind,
secret turbulence.

Fraught, eclipsed, the mind's night face. Dark field
between two bodies, the chill – clinging
to a crazed refrain, remembering.

A child's need to number the shadows on her bedroom wall,
tangled in her clothes. In the harbour, slow boats loading,
unloading stars.

First frost, inner leaves curled against the cold. Cornhusks,
compost of eggshells and dreams. A rot,
a sweetness lingering.

Four

# More Light

# Folding

I

*In some origamic*
*paradise*    red cranes,
a child's blue boat folded,
cupped in a palm.

We huddle over paper fortunes –
pick a colour, a number,
a star –

you will marry a gypsy,
a pauper, a god,
you will have nothing,
hold the heavens in your arms.

*The creased waves* rustle,
silk over sand    molluscs,
polished glass, crabs
in their mirror worlds

as under the weedy stone,
one last tissue layer –

a trace and its green shadow
fold in *a deeper embrace*.

No, never a final word –
the corners peeled back, revelation
of the empty word.

*The edge of joy, the edge*
*of melancholy,* unending
witness
        seawrack, salt carnage,
veins, vesicles of light –
constellations in a teardrop.

You have seen your life
        fold inward, leaf by leaf,
and the gift at the centre
is laughter.

Wave upon wave
        *you must fold*
*your hands,* breathe a prayer
for the little boat blown,
unfolding
        out to sea.

2

The moon is almost full, drinking
light      laughing belly, buddha
of clarities.

In the articulate heart, forms
fan open
          sickle wind,
a flame's tusk flaying.

Just this folding, shapely
interlacing, breath by trembling
breath
          my words
rapt in the scent, skin
of what you are.

Wind in its syllables – words,
cloud-tressed, blow silvered
or dim
          in the fissured heart,
forms leaf into being,
no release
          from this rending.

A ghost is caught in the fold-
ing, weft and tearing,
love
     its *continuous song*
is our song, wandering,

lost in *the unfolded of what we are.*

3

*And I will come to you, and make*
*my dwelling with you.*

In May evenings, when new leaves
are polished gold, clouds
take the colour of imperfection –
purple, a dusky ink
signed with a flourish,
splendid.

Words stream on the wind, quick
and dying.

Hers was the first garden –
rain, always rain,
pink dogwood by the window,
forsythia in yellow sprays.
Her hands wet
among stars, her face
erased by light.

*Where words foment*
*a largeness*, where the warmth
of spring, supple skin
of this moment – dispersed,
love's elegiac, slow
unfurling.

The dying sun is grafted
in the heart, just a slip,
tissue of blessings.

If light had a shape, it would be
that young fern curled
in your palm, that lily
figuring sleep.

Sun and shadow enfold us,
nimbus, brief
entangling
        *the Beloved*
*is the murmur at the edge*
        birds startle at her kiss,
fleeing.

4

Fluid mother, vortices
of words
          the folds of the soul
are lined with stars
     what else
can I say.

Tracing hollows in the hours
days fold into twilight
          apples, sparrows
into cloud.

White forms within forms
          one bean
               ivory earring
stream of ooooooo's
snowflakes
on a curving wind

and fingers ply the hours
thread
          by purple thread
knotted in the heart –
gold-veined,
a few winter rooftops.

Folds of wind
and water, such dreams
involutions –
            rose nacre,
the spiral of your ear
                the sea's far tongues,
the maelstroms.

# Sshhh

You lie breathing in the dark, one breast still wet with milk, the baby finally tucked away in his crib. Shower of hail against the window, a far-off siren. You imagine the coloured lights lifting off the river.

Spent, you have gathered up the scraps, piecing them into a story too thin, barely holding – and nothing left of this mourning but to begin again, there is always another scene, it emerges shining from the inner fold of the day, rosy, smooth like the shells you would pick up off the beach as a child, holding them to your ear, listening, *sshhh*. You will never forget those muttered words, the sea's low moan, *dead, dead*. Grief covers the earth, a gulf of nascent words – *swell, billow, flood, now sanctify these waters* – and under the drone a terror whiter than knuckle, stone. There is always another scene, imprint of a secret –

child shivering in the rising tide –

# The Return

Wind enters the room as you comb the debris on another shore. Thought's flotsam, sticks and barnacle rocks, the bitter cut of tears.  Something sings in the sea, and the waves roll over and over, a swell, *houle*. A child rises to the surface and floats on the foam, hair green as weeds, mouth a small hole, O! of surprise.

Tentacle fingers, the anemone's quick touch – purpled, rosy as a baby's blood. The child has returned, her skin covered with kisses, pearly in the morning light. *Let me go back to the sea, that soft bed deeper than grieving.* The foam sparkles on her hair as she turns with a little flick of her tail, and dives –

a windchill, windows tremble in the sudden gust, early summer duststorm, lossssssst – *I am you child, your disappearing years        turn around, we can almost        touch*

# Equinox

1

*After paradise, we enter the beginning of memory.* The gate opens, shuts; a child disappears behind the hedge. Quick glimpse of red curls among the sunflowers. Illuminations: a fountain spilling, delicate tangle of daisies. Time halts. A finger turns a page in the clouds. The child reappears, moving purposefully, head bent. She pauses at the gate, lifts the latch.

2

*Humans are always at the door of paradise, on the point of losing it and not inside.* The gate opens both ways. In the centre of the garden, a tree flames bright as a sword. The child is sleepy, and lies down to rest, a host of sunflowers bending over her. In the garden, she is free. The gate opens. She is safe, she is not. Safe, not. A little grief scratches in the dust.

3

This morning, a first chill. Exhalations hang in the trees, our breath disappears into the sun. This is the minimal moment, this point where light and time meet. Skeletal time. The cat's underground, buried with a jam jar of messages: 'Love me, gather me, feed me.' In every garden a little grave, pale angel hovering over hollyhocks. Raspberry bushes heavy with rotting fruit. Emaciated children, nameless babies at the gate.

## 4

An early snow bows the wheat. We dream of Europe, its castles and faery forests. A child is lost, endlessly retracing her path. The killer raises a cigarette delicately to his lips, white fingers in fingerless black gloves. In the sudden hush we think of love, our terrible passion for children. September dreams filled with sun, yet each morning's frost a little darker. Stone round the neck, a few ripples in the river, geese flying frightened out of the north.

## 5

Autumn compost, cornsilk, a few stripped husks. Kitchen gardens dripping in the rain. Yellow leaves, the cat underground down to one eye, a few black bones. Bleak harvest, heap of broken sunflowers. The child is crying at the bottom of the garden, her striped dress caught in the gate. We walk under clouds, imagining sun, that hand tossing the chaff away. His flaming sleeve, strong arm for the final binding.

# If We Fall

The end comes out of shadow. The neighbour spreads straw mulch against a late frost. In a barren garden, I sit reading poem after poem, seeking the word for immolation. Heaven's cataclysm, doors up and down the street fly open, houses lightwashed. If we fall we shall catch larks, spiralling to the chimneytops like last year's leaves, newspapers, sleeves escaped from a washline. African orphans, a scrap, slain, flown away. A whole world shivers in this machete wind, our children's bodies fodder for some final story. Ruddy moon, ochrous light.

# More Light

Time is seamless. September sun lucid in the leaves, hearts pump-
ing some fine, transparent spirit tinged with green. At night the half
moon puts out sails – we cycle after it, our bikes clattering. Quiet
conversations punctuate the dusk. Once, in your arms lit by earth-
light, I experienced the brief illumination of the foolish and dying.
The dark enfolds us daily, leaving only a thin wafer of sun under
our tongues. Yet we put on our coats and step out, avoiding cracks
in the pavement, scattering the crumbs of our happiness. Raptors
with razor tails skim from elm to elm. Where does the dark end?
Thought cuts away – in the magpie laughter of this brilliant month
we sense the dead gaping behind every tree. Combines work the
fields past midnight, dew falls. In the silence, mice. We will lie
down in the chaff, death in our arms, and sleep in the moon's deri-
sion. Whether waking or the testament of birds.

# Diptych

## Night

Breathing, darkness curls around the body of thought. Nerves entwine in small of back, spine, the cranium's glowing sphere. The northern lights stretch over the pole, white vertebrae numbered one by one. Far below, little chimneys with their tresses of smoke. A rosy body imprinted on the retina, each cell lit up from within, *lux*, you shall have and have in abundance. Far-flung beacons dot the prairie, its indigo curves, folds. Swift illusions cross our faces, windows ignite in morning sun.

The slightest exhalation, tracing the night path of birds or angels. This melancholy, a field of pewter leaves. A river runs through the heart, and somewhere the luminous estuary. Bruised skies, the goddess' sleeve brushes the land, its frozen spine. A volatile *cloud of unknowing*. A dream-dragon coils over the snowy plain – the flux and muscle of a cold jade heart. Areola, veined tongue of the rose, love's secret imprint in cell and plasm. Morning licks a pink finger, turns a page.

## L'Aube

It might be the way a single star appears each morning, the way breath flowers, miraculous, on the cold pane. Hands on warm belly, eyes on the east. Dawn with its chill palette: freshet, icefloe, hoarflower, rime. Iris streaked with gold, transparent hands gild the trees. You wait, breath suspended, in the clarity of too much love, light breaking over your head, over the somnolent body of the world.

So far from earth, wings in perpetual motion. The naked eye discerns petals, asterisks, luminous fish. Nocturnal blooms under glass. Lovers wake, shivering: faults, blue tongues in the ice. Mother of pearl, the orient rising. Light unfurls, brushing cortex, shaft, ramifying nerve. Joy a small death, imprint of kisses on throat and hands, windows glazed in rose, flame.

Metallic, a quiver of fine quills. Waking in the god's eye, corolla, flash of silver scales. Bed damp with love, the mollusc's white, lustrous seed. Magpies scream harsh albas in the cold, and you lie, listening: river ice crying, tongued water, desire. Bodies licked with pain, flesh etched with little mouths – you cry out in loss, a sky consumed, resurrection.

# Intervals

I

To sink into sleep, tracing the vein
on your wrist, stripped
moonlight –

intimacy of hollows, rose-prints
on the skin –

a life, a signature creased,
folded
        licks of thunder,
dusky intervals between leaves.

Moths swoon in the shadows
and other guests,
flickering.

2

*Lachrymae christi*, purple sails
in the heavens.

What would it be to write light,
streaked
                tulips weeping
on their stems?

Stress of love or air
about us, skin bereft –
such tongues –
                as if the very stones would shiver,
split.

Death slips among the leaves, brief
wings and nocturnes,
ghostly.

3

A strong wine of spit
and tears –
                    we are robed
in reflection, flesh stricken
in every glass.

Impelled in our syllables, wind's
reminiscence –

discerning that trace or musk
in the next garden,
feather, sinew, tongues racked
and singing.

Twilight scales, arpeggios
of the darkening heart, such messengers.

# We Come to Dwell

*Into the dark beyond all light we pray*
*to come ...*
     – Pseudo-Dionysius


     I


In the beginning, a child's word shines
on a beloved face. A window washed with tears.

We come to dwell in the folds and holes
between syllables. Recessed, shaped by the unsaid,
unthought.

No, light is little in the garden of loss
and endless attending.

Golden, we are loved by the dusk,
cup brief flames in our hands.

Memory's involutions –
the cursor a small heart beating
on spectral ground.

Raven wing, moon:
words slope off into the woods.

2

*The light shines in the darkness,*
a match struck over a sleeping face.

We dwell in the ripples and wavelets
of thought. Dark muscle, bitter birth.

No passage back, calyx and curling vine,
a fine green rain slanting into the tomb.

We turn the page, drawn into the twilight
between words. What hollows, what waves?

There are voices in the garden – *oh list,*
throstle lost, glistening threads
spun leaf to leaf.

Love's hairsbreadth – always dusk,
this hunger.

3

Radiant knots, our final words are darkness,
utter clarity.

A dawn of songbirds and severed limbs,
a ground mined with unknowing.

This is the eclipse of memory:
we dwell in the shards and remains of the new.

Wanting the midwife, her terrible hands.
Our limbs knit, unravelled
in laughter.

New songs in a conch shell –
tritons rise crying from the waves.

Words wet as pebbles under foam,
and the surge,
and something withdrawing.

# Hallowed

Light's forelock, slim knot of asphyxiation and laughter. Something falls, and in the festive nervous riot dinning this holy night, a marriage of eros and fear. Fear soft as snow, as the amorous flakes nuzzling the dark windows. Fear in our throats as we climb the stairs, kissing, breathless. Probing the word *excess*, its velvety folds. Tasting synonyms – *surfeit, satiety, hunger* – tongues honeysweet, peevish. Joy chills our lips. Spent, we sleep as angels pull back the veil from the stars. This night, as old men gather bitter herbs, resins, and gold, the cries of famished infants cleave our dreams. This gift, apprehension of sickle and wing.

# New Snow

In the end, a small bird released, bright ribs and a plumage beyond the bluest imagination. Thinking in a shower of new snow. Paradise is this garden, perfection of fern, clover, star. Orders of angels compacted in each snowflake – a boy licks his mittens, an explosion of hymns. Love arrives quickly with black-tipped wings and a quiver of icicles, warning us away. Forty years of winter light. White apples fall, frozen, to the earth

and the human animal foolish, anomalous, covered with flowers. Vision petalled, crystals starring our eyes. This is my wish: that the arctic heart turn again, a faint path traced, effaced in blowing snow. Tipsy scuffles in the rowan tree, scarlet berries at our feet.

# Little Births

This is the child: a small boy grabs his shadow in his crib. He laughs, dazzled, in the morning light. This is the child: an older boy stands in a doorway, clutching his white robes, squinting at the AK 47 just visible around the building's corner.

This morning, the air forms crystals on our tongues. The river cracks and shivers, sun pink and distant. Little births, a flame folded in each snowflake, white envelopes tucked into mailboxes. In the bleak bushes, wings – premonitions of light. Heart agitated, caught up like a paper fan.

Peace, the child is frozen, forever drawing his white robes around him, forever on the threshold, facing the soldier with the rifle, breath rising in plumes, as light dawns on a numb and sleeping world.

*That my flesh be enfolded in flame*, a thin skin between eyes and light. Stars fall from the sky, their molten glass cracking in the snow. This is my gift, this gold band I twist and twist on my finger. Fire on the horizon, columns of smoke, the babe crying, cold and hungry in his mother's thin arms. Herod's warriors cry out, a holy war!  And it is done, the bodies of yearlings burning in midnight fires all over the world, explosions in the night sky as something precious dies, a gift, a little love.

My babies, two waxy dolls. When I have finished playing with them, I put them away in a drawer, tucking their swaddling clothes around them, blowing on their blue cheeks. As I slide the drawer in, I can hear their stifled cries.

Frost-ferns pattern the attic window. I blow a peep-hole with my breath. From the top of the house, I can see for miles. Neat homes in rows, smoke rising in white feathers. I would like to pick the little houses up, put them in my pockets, shush the mothers and babies, stop their cries. Tiny dogs run wildly up and down the streets, barking into the still air.

Crystals, an iridescence. Something silent forming. I turn to my babies, drawing the snowy sheets over their heads. Wings brush the window; beyond, two stars. Snow in my empty hands.

4

On New Year's Day, there were snow squalls off Lake Superior. The men going on ahead found a frozen baby under the ice. It looked like a newborn, blue. In places where the sky had fallen in, the men broke up the shards as they walked away.

I dream of a warming, Canada geese on the wing. The heat of the sun breaks up the lake as I lean over the child, lift it from its loose mantle of ice. She is as small as my little finger, a prawn blooming pink under my breath. I put her to my breast, one drop of milk, then another, forming, flowing in the general thaw.

# Notes

I would like to thank Tim Lilburn and Anne Szumigalski for their early encouragement and their comments on the manuscript, and Marnie Parsons and Don McKay of Brick Books for their fine editorial work.

'Basho's Dream' incorporates fragments from Basho's *The Narrow Road to the Deep North*, transl. Noboyuki Yuasa (Penguin, 1966).

'Swallows' and 'Dance' are based on Eugenio Montale's 'The soaring-dipping white and black' and 'Bagni di Lucca' in *The Occasions*, transl. William Arrowsmith (Norton, 1987).

The poems in 'Luminous' are based on poems in Robin Blaser's 'The Moth Poem', *The Holy Forest* (Coach House Press, 1993).

The phrase 'torn birds' in 'Woman in Doorway (Variations)' is Erin Mouré's in *Sheepish Beauty, Civilian Love* (Véhicule Press, 1992).

The phrase 'optic heart' in 'Testament' is Margaret Avison's in 'Snow', *Margaret Avison: Selected Poems* (Oxford Univ. Press, 1991).

The poems in 'Her' incorporate fragments from Normand de Bellefeuille's *Categorics*, transl. D.G. Jones (Coach House Press, 1992).

In 'Woman Bathing', 'Hale Akela' refers to the volcano on the island of Maui.

'Folding' (1) incorporates fragments from Don Domanski's 'The God of Folding', *Stations of the Left Hand* (Coach House Press, 1994).

'Folding' (2) incorporates fragments from Robin Blaser's 'Letter to a Student', *The Capilano Review* (Spring 1994).

'Folding' (3) includes fragments from Robin Blaser's *The Holy Forest* (Coach House Press, 1993).

'Equinox' #1 and #2 include sentences from Hélène Cixous' *Readings* (Univ. of Minnesota Press, 1991).

'Little Births' (2) includes a phrase from *Beowulf*, transl. E. Talbot Donaldson (Norton, 1966).

# Acknowledgements

Some of the poems in *More Light* have appeared in the following journals: *CV2, raddle moon, The New Quarterly, Capilano Review, Malahat Review, The Fiddlehead* and *Grain*.

Hilary Clark lives in Saskatoon, where she teaches English and Women's Studies at the University of Saskatchewan. Her work has appeared in such journals as *Writing, CV2, raddle moon, Grain* and *Malahat Review*. *More Light* is her first book. She has also written *Two Heavens*, a book of poems soon to be published by Hagios Press.